A PEASANT OF EL SALVADOR

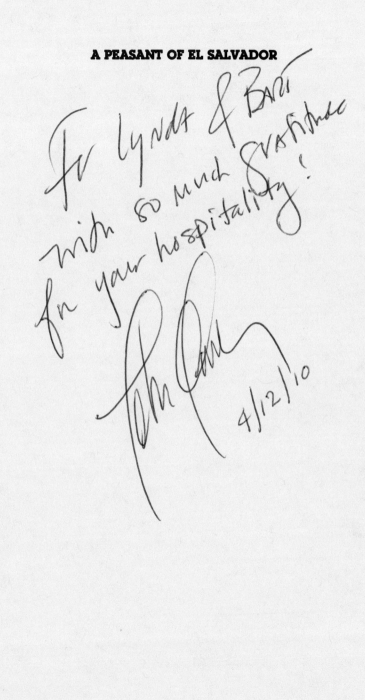

For Lynda & Bart
with so much gratitude
for your hospitality!

4/12/10

By the same author
BURNT TOAST
(A.A. Knopf, 1971)

A Peasant
of
El Salvador

A Play by
Peter Gould
developed for the stage by
Peter Gould and **Stephen Stearns**

WHETSTONE BOOKS
Brattleboro, Vermont

Second Printing October 1984
Third Printing (Specially dedicated to the Sanctuary Movement)
September 1985

Book design by Ed Helminski

All photographs taken by Jim Sielicki: Gould & Stearns in performance at the Ritz Theatre, Tiffin, Ohio, October, 1983.

Manufactured in the United States of America

WHETSTONE BOOKS
22 West St.
Brattleboro Vt. 05301

Distributed in the United Kingdom by
Writers and Readers Publishing Cooperative
144 Camden High Street
London NW1 ONE

CONTENTS

INTRODUCTION

Last night, I witnessed a performance of "A Peasant of El Salvador." I wept as I watched the unfolding of this story of a humble man caught in the inexorable process of liberation. It is painful to observe, and yet — paradoxically, a cleansing and healing experience.

"A Peasant of El Salvador" is a simple tale, told simply but with candor and feeling by two very accomplished artists. Obviously presented with love, it is a gradual and tender unwrapping of the story of a peasant — a little man, though somehow much larger than life.

Gould and Stearns, in an hour, tell that same story which so many have sought to relate. Deftly, and with bold, sure strokes, they outline the personal involvement of this little man, who really is *Everyman*, in a struggle which neither he nor the rich and powerful really understand.

"A Peasant of El Salvador" moves on with the momentum of a Greek tragedy. We were witnesses to — and accomplices in — the story. By inviting the audience to take part, Gould and Stearns enabled us to recognize our role and our complicity, even, in the tragedy called "El Salvador."

This was a powerful experience, used well by two very talented and feeling people. Thank God for "A Peasant of El Salvador" and for folks like Gould and Stearns.

Rev. Daniel P. Jensen
Maryknoll,
June 21, 1982

*We dedicate our drama to Archbishop Oscar Romero,
Maura Clarke, Ita Ford, Dorothy Kazel, Jean Donovan,
Victor Jara, Salvador Allende, and all the "desaparecidos,"
the disappeared ones in their unmarked graves.*

"A Peasant of El Salvador" was first performed at St. Michael's
Church, Brattleboro, Vermont, on April 12, 1981. Commissioned
by Father Seamus Finn to commemorate Monseñor Oscar
Romero's murder, it was created and performed solo by Peter
Gould. Since then, it has been re-designed for a two-man
company:

> FIRST ACTOR
>
> Narrator One
> Manuel
> Crop Foreman
> Comandante
> Raul
> U.S. Government Spokesman
> Salvadoran Officer
> Wealthy Landowner
> Archbishop Romero
> Boy
> Soldier
> News Broadcaster
>
> SECOND ACTOR
>
> Narrator Two
> Jesús (*pronounced Hay-soos*)
> Television montage
> Prison Guard

This edition makes the play available for performance by companies
of any size. Please see "NOTES BY THE AUTHOR," page 42.

"A Peasant of El Salvador" was first performed in Great Britain by Gould and Stearns from November 29 to December 3, 1983 as a part of the Greater London Council's International Year of Peace. The engagement, at three London cultural centers, St. James Cathedral, and the London School of Economics, was organized by the El Salvador Committee for Human Rights, and managed by the Theatre Company 7:84.

A village in El Salvador, about 1975. A narrow (six-foot wide) colored backdrop suggests a stucco house. In front, two low stools on a straw mat. Hanging on the backdrop, miscellaneous gear: a machete, a hemp bag, some torn hats, lengths of rope, last year's palm branch, an interesting feather. An old broom, leaning.

Extreme front right, a low table with cloth and votive candles, suggesting a poor church interior.

Enter JESÚS *(Hay-soos) and* NARRATOR ONE *as music comes up.* *
JESÚS wears straw hat, peasant white pants and shirt, NARRATOR *in Latin-American student garb. Both carry various hats and props indicating characters to appear later. They hang them on the backdrop, or rest them behind the stools, as* JESÚS's *voice, speaking Spanish, is heard, also on tape, over the music. As his speech changes to English, they form a tableau, holding until the voice-over ends.*

ACT I

JESÚS (*Voice-Over*): Yo tengo mi fé. Yo sé que ellos, que el gobierno puede quitar todo. Me puede quitar mi casa, mi esposa, mis hijos, mi milpa, mi trabajo, mi vida. Pero tengo la seguridad que al fin hay una cosa que no me pueden quitar — y eso es: mi salvación.

I know that the government can take away everything. They can take my house, my wife, my children, my piece of ground, my work, even my life. But I know also that at the end there is one thing they can't take away, and that is: my salvation. Look —up there on the hill behind the house: there is the piece of land that used to be mine. Yo voy a explicarle todo. I am going to tell you how I lost that land.

*See Discography, page 44.

1

A Peasant of El Salvador

(JESÚS sweeping his dooryard. Low Andean bamboo pipe & guitar are playing as background.)

NARRATOR ONE: Not long ago, in a country called El Salvador, which means in English "The Savior," there lived a man named Hay-soos, which in English we would pronounce "Jesus."

Now Jesús (Hay-soos) was a very poor man. He lived with his wife, Concepción, who worked sometimes beside him in the fields, but she usually stayed in the house. They had four children almost grown, and a young boy who had come to them late in life. Three other children had died before the age of two. They lived in a beautiful country that was peaceful and green all the year round — eh, Jesús?

JESÚS: Sí, aquí se puede vivir muy bien: Well, if you work hard, you can have a good life here. To be poor in the countryside, where you can grow your own food, breathe the good air, and not work for somebody else, that is not so bad.

NARRATOR ONE: Jesús and his family lived in a little village called San Pedro El Pacífico, St. Peter the Peaceful, or, St. Peter near the Pacific. You can see it clinging to the mountainside here —

JESÚS: Over there is the tiny grocery store. It's the only one in town. You see the sign above the door. Este, uh —

NARRATOR ONE: He doesn't read. (*To* JESÚS): TOME COCA COLA.

JESÚS: Sí. TO-ME CO-CA CO-LA.

NARRATOR ONE: Inside, you see the dusty bottles of Alka-Seltzair and Veeks Vahporube.

JESÚS (*entering church*): This is the stone church, where everybody in town comes to pray —

NARRATOR ONE: They come more than once a week. Now, we are standing in a plaza. Oh, it doesn't really deserve the name of plaza. There's an old Spanish fountain, but it's been dry since the Spanish left. Up there is a basketball rim, with no net, high on a pole. The pole is made of concrete.

JESÚS: No hay luz y fuerza.

NARRATOR ONE: How's that?

JESÚS: No tenemos luz!

NARRATOR ONE: Ah! There is no electricity. Nowhere in the village. Hasn't even come close. At the back of the plaza are four or five houses, all built of adobe brick, covered with stucco, painted, scrubbed once a year — you can see them gleaming in the tropical mountain sun. In front of each house is a farmyard, surrounded by a wall of piled-up stones. Within the yard, you might find a turkey, a skinny dog, some chickens, (*Here* JESÚS *mimes stalking a hen, catching it suddenly; then, magically, he finds a real egg in his hand*):

JESÚS: Hoy vamos a comer! Today we are going to eat.

NARRATOR ONE: . . . also some potted plants, a stone bench, a pomegranate tree, and a pile of dried-up corn stalks to feed to the animals.

(JESÚS *exits. He returns with an enamel water pitcher, stretching as if from work-stiffness.*)

NARRATOR ONE: When the day's work ended, Jesús and his family did not go to the movies. They didn't watch TV. They didn't even read books. In El Salvador, more than half the people have never had a chance to learn how to read. Instead, they found joy in each other. Jesús, as the sun went down, would sit on his bench under the pomegranate tree, and watch his kids playing soccer in the street. That was their soccerball court.

(*The actors cry out various street sounds.* NARRATOR ONE *pretends he is one of* JESÚS's *sons playing ball. He runs, kicks, seems to score a goal.*)

NARRATOR ONE: Goal!

JESÚS (*looking carefully, frowning*): No. Fuera! Lo ví. It was out.

NARRATOR ONE: Papá! Cómo que nó? Goal! — Or, he would watch his six-year-old boy, Juancito, shooting his slingshot at the stars as they came out, one by one. (NARRATOR ONE *mimes this action.*) He really believed that if he hit one, it would fall into the dirt; he could wash it off in the stream and put it in his pocket.

(NARRATOR *picks up hat, glasses, guitar, becoming* MANUEL *as he says*): Or sometimes Manuel, the one man in the village who owned a halfway decent guitar, would stop by and sing a song or two. When he was home from the university.

MANUEL: Jesús! Compa! How are you?

JESÚS: Manuel! Pása-le.

MANUEL: Jesús, I got a song for you.

JESÚS: A new one? (*To the audience*): He always plays the same song.

MANUEL: Well, it's a new arrangement. (*He plays a very familiar Latin American song, like "La Bamba." JESÚS gestures, "See, I told you" to the audience, then dances energetically until he tires.*)

JESÚS: Basta.

NARRATOR ONE: (*Removing* MANUEL *costume and prop*): But the thing that gave Jesús the most pleasure was his little plot of ground. You see it there, high on the hillside above the village? It had been in his family for two hundred years. It was theirs. Jesús loved that plot of ground. Turning over the same soil that his forefathers had tilled for generations before him, he didn't know it, but Victor Jara, the famous Chilean folksinger, had written a song about a man just like him. . . .

(*Victor Jara's song, El Arado, comes on, on tape. First, the short instrumental intro, heard while* JESÚS *mimes climbing the steep hill to his land and putting his hands on his plow. Then the words:*)

> Aprieto firme mi mano
> Y hundo el arado en la tierra
> hace años que llevo en ella
> como no estar agotado.
> Vuelan mariposas, cantan grillos
> la piel se me pone negra
> y el sol brilla, brilla, brilla
> el sudor me hace surcos,
> yo hago surcos a la tierra sin parar. . . .)

NARRATOR ONE: (*translating while* JESÚS *mimes three farming motions: pushing the plow, hoe-ing, and planting seed with a tall dibble stick*): "I steady my hand, and sink my plow into the earth; for many years I've worked her, as if she were not worn out. . . . The sun beats down, turning my skin to black; the sweat makes furrows in my brow, just as my plow makes furrows in the earth. . . ."

NARRATOR TWO: (*as* JESÚS's *earth-tending movements end*): Now Jesús's plot of ground was too steep to plow by machine. In fact, he often used to joke about the blackbirds that might have come to steal his corn. He'd say:

JESÚS: Blackbirds? They'd never land on my plot! Want to know why? — they're too afraid they might fall off!

5

NARRATOR TWO: Yes, his land was steep, and full of rocks, but it brought forth a good crop because the soil was volcanic and the sun was strong, and if you didn't turn it over too deeply in the springtime, it wouldn't all wash away when the rains came.

In this plot of ground Jesús grew corn. But not the big, golden, juicy ears of sweet corn that we love to sink our teeth into for a summertime treat. No. The kind of corn Jesús grew was stunted and irregular: the kernels were orange, red, blue, black: the kind of corn that, if we were to find it growing in our garden, we might throw it away, or stick it up on the wall as a curiosity. We certainly wouldn't know how to cook it. But to Jesús it was life. It was 12% protein, and it was non-hybrid corn, which meant that you could save the seed from year to year to plant, and you'd always get the same corn. It was resistant to drought, to heavy rain, to sun scald, and very dependable: no expensive fertilizers needed.

This corn made a delicious drink, or bread, or tortilla. And when you mixed it with black beans, frijoles negros, it gave you a complete protein: maíz y frijoles, corn and beans! Now the people of El Salvador had been eating this complete protein for a thousand years, long before Nutritional Science told them it was the right thing to do.

NARRATOR ONE: Jesús didn't have enough land to grow beans, but that didn't matter. Beans were cheap in those days, grown and sold by the market farmers down below, where the land was flatter. You could plant a long, straight row there. The farmers could irrigate with the water that washed down the mountainsides, or they could afford to pump water from deep in the ground. They had tractors; they could farm bigger parcels efficiently. So for not very much money Jesús could buy the beans, put them with the corn, and he and his wife Concepción, they put a nice meal on the table for the kids, and a little left over for themselves —

JESÚS: Poquito! (*very little!*)

NARRATOR ONE: — and they didn't suffer.

JESÚS: Tell the truth —

NARRATOR ONE: Well, most years they didn't suffer. At least Jesús had some land. And things might have gone on this way for a long time, had it not been that one thing changed: the price of beans began slowly to go up. Jesús didn't complain. He was not the sort of man who complained. He just thought to himself:

JESÚS: Debe de haber algo que puedo hacer para ganar dinero . . .

NARRATOR ONE: There has to be something I can do to earn some money. Then he thought of it. (JESÚS *mimes the insight and the following action:*) Two or three mornings a week, he would leave his house before dawn, hike out back, up a twisting, stony path past his plot of ground, and up to where the land leveled off, a plateau, from where he could see the Pacific Ocean, stretching far away to the south . . .

JESÚS (*pointing*): There it is; look how beautiful —

NARRATOR TWO: (*while* JESÚS *mimes flower-cutting*): This was his favorite spot on earth. And here grew a profusion of wildflowers, which Jesús would pick when the dew was still fresh on the petals. He'd pack them into an old cardboard box, put the box on his back and the strap around his forehead, and head back down the twisted trail.

NARRATOR ONE: It was a nine-mile hike to the nation's capital. San Salvador. The Holy Savior.

NARRATOR TWO: There, in the immemorial marketplace, Jesús would find a spot among all the other vendors gathered to hawk their wares:

BOTH NARRATORS (*taking turns*): Cacahuates! Chocolate! Lana! Leña! Melón! Sandía! Mandarinas! Verduras! Tortillas! Plátanos! Pescado frito!

NARRATOR TWO: Jesús would add his own cry to the din:

JESÚS: Flores! Tengo Flores! I've got flowers!

NARRATOR TWO (*while* JESÚS *mimes*): Mornings when Jesús was feeling particularly chipper, he wouldn't go to the marketplace. He'd walk right by. He'd cross the great plaza where the cathedral stood —

JESÚS: Que bonito, no? Someday they going to finish it.

NARRATOR TWO: He would hike across town to the wealthy suburbs, where they had the big stucco houses, behind the stone walls with the broken glass along the top. And the iron gates through which he could see the flashy American cars. He'd knock on the doors:

JESÚS (*in the audience, knocking on aisle seats*): Flores? You want some flowers? (*Holding out his hand for money*): Y para mí: gracias. Flores frescas— fresh flowers; acabo de cortarlas. Gracias.

(JESÚS *goes to three people in the audience, knocking humbly, pretending to sell flowers and accept coins.*)

NARRATOR TWO: And when he'd sold his whole crop, when he had his little handful of cash, he would stop at the marketplace, buy the beans for his family; then he'd hike the nine miles back to San Pedro el Pacífico.

NARRATOR ONE: He didn't know it, but sometimes after he left those big clean houses with the iron gates and the fancy cars, the people behind the shuttered windows would chuckle to each other about how cheaply he had sold those flowers, gathered in the early dawn and borne on his back down the twisting path. And they'd say, someday the old man is gonna find out. But the years went by, and Jesús never did.

Meanwhile the price of beans went higher. And higher. But Jesús didn't complain. He was not the sort of man to complain —

JESÚS: No importa, digo. It doesn't matter. I'll get up earlier — I could go up there every day of the week. Two boxes of flowers. Maybe I'll get a job below and spend less time on my land. My sons can take care of it. Soy fuerte y podemos aguantar. I'm strong, and we'll get by. Hey—maybe we eat too much anyway.

NARRATOR TWO: But that spring when he went down to the fields in the valley he saw why it was that the price of beans had gone up 200% that year:

JESÚS (*gazing out toward the fields*): Por todos lados, no hay frijoles.

NARRATOR TWO: — as far as he could see, there was not a single bean plant growing. He saw many different kinds of food crops, but they were not the kind of food that he or his family, his kids, ever had a chance to eat. A foreman who worked there — El Exigente — explained it to him:

FOREMAN: No Old Man, we don't grow beans here any more. We're eatin' meat now. Hey, our beans weren't so good anyway. You want a bag of beans, though, I can sell you a much better one now. We import them now from Texas. California. Producto de U.S.A.! They got a much higher quality up there and they harvest by machine. No, Old Man, you see what we grow here now: sugar cane, check it out, check it out, Man — (*taps Jesús in the stomach*)

JESÚS: Si, caña —

FOREMAN: The people in Cheecago, Massa-choo-seets, Escarsdale, _____ (*naming the town where the play is being performed*), they got a sweet tooth. They want their sugar cane, their bananas, their coffee, especially their strawberries in the winter time. They pay me any price I ask: even if I double it, they still pay. So it makes good business sense, no? I can make a lot more money selling these crops to them than I can selling beans to you! Besides, you don't have enough money to pay me what I need to get for my work.

But hey, I tell you what: someday you gonna need a job, no? You come see me. I put you to work.

JESÚS: Ah, gracias. (*He offers his hand.*)

FOREMAN: De nada. (*He does not shake the hand.*) I gotta go. Adiós.

NARRATOR TWO (*As* JESÚS *walks off*): Jesús did not understand business. In fact, he did not understand very much of what went on in the world outside San Pedro el Pacífico. (*Exit* JESÚS.)

NARRATOR ONE: Jesús only vaguely knew that El Salvador was controlled by fourteen wealthy families, closely inter-married with the military. But he didn't know that they had gained their wealth and power by taking advantage of people like himself. Now they were becoming afraid that they might lose everything. So they had bought tanks, helicopter gunships, repeating rifles, napalm leftover from Vietnam, uniforms for their soldiers, guards, and security police — and all these items, manufactured and sold by the United States of America, cost a lot of money. So they were going into export agriculture to keep up with the balance of payments. You all know what that means? Well: it means that you no longer grow the staple crops, the corn and beans, that your neighbors and good friends need to eat. Now you grow something more exotic, for someone who lives far away, who has a lot more money to pay you. Makes good business sense, yes?

Jesús didn't know this. He also didn't know that the families still were nervous. They thought, maybe it's not such a good idea to have all our money tied up in land — what if we should lose it by land reform or revolution? They decided to industrialize, and they invited United States advisors down to show them how to run their plants and corporations. Now when these advisors packed up and went home, many of the new manufacturing corporations were owned, in large part, by companies with headquarters in New York or Texas. The wealthy families were better off than ever: they had their Swiss bank accounts, condominiums in Miami Beach; in fact, they lived at a level of luxury that we here can hardly imagine!

(NARRATOR *produces a chart*):

They had made an arrangement with these foreign corporations. They agreed not to impose any taxes on profits for the first ten years. They would hold the wages of the Salvadoran workers down near 15¢ an hour. They promised to outlaw unions and strikes, and not to pass any of those silly environmental laws that make it so hard for a company to make an honest profit. They said they'd look the other way when the workers were forced to handle toxic chemicals and sprays in lethal amounts with no protective clothing. They told the foreign corporations, we'll help you market your stockpiles of banned

9

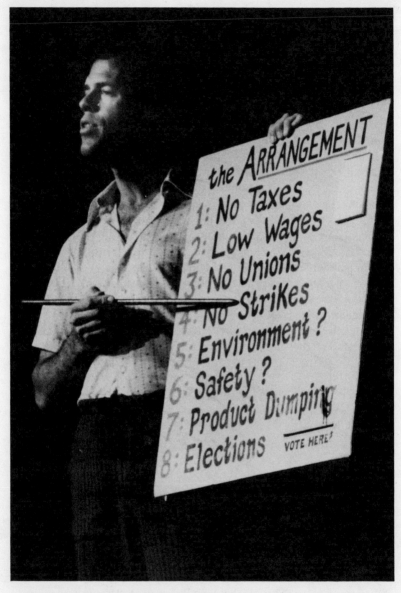

products, the DDT, the Dalkon shields, the fire-resistant baby-clothes, that you can no longer sell, by law, in the United States. We'll help you sell them right here in Salvador.

And finally, (JESÚS *re-appears, in a mime of voting in a polling place. The chart has a slot for his X-marked card.*) they vowed to hold elections very soon, and frequently, so that the folks in the U.S.A. would know that El Salvador had always been moderate and democratic. (JESÚS's *vote falls to the ground;* NARRATOR ONE *picks it up, crumbles it, tosses it.*)

NARRATOR TWO (*as* JESÚS *returns to his plow*): No, Jesús did not know this. Not any of it. All that he knew was:

JESÚS: Pues, los frijoles son muy caros. The beans are very expensive. Well, no importa, eh? It doesn't matter. Tengo mi fe: I have my faith, and I know that if I work hard que todo va a cambiar, that everything's going to change —

NARRATOR ONE (*rushing up to* JESÚS's *plot of ground*): Things did change, but, they got worse! (*Whispers to* JESÚS; JESÚS *rushes back to his house.*) You remember Jesús's little boy, Juancito? Well, he became ill. It was just a simple fever: our children would throw it off in a day or two. But for Juancito it was different; he was malnourished; his body was weak. The fever consumed him and he died. This was a terrible blow for Jesús. Juancito, his youngest, was his joy. (JESÚS *comes out of his house, slowly, hat off.*) Never again, he thought, would he see his boy smile.

JESÚS: Que nunca más voy a ver su sonrisa tan ancha —

NARRATOR ONE: Nor watch his little feet kicking the soccer ball —

JESÚS: Jugando al futbol, o tirando a las estrellas, Juancito Tiradora —

NARRATOR ONE: Watch him shoot his slingshot at the stars . . . He took his last peso and went to the church to light a candle, to speed his son's soul onward.

JESÚS (*at prayer, lighting first candle*): Padre nuestro, que estás *en los cielos, sanctificado sea tu nombre* —

NARRATOR ONE: Now Jesús was not a talkative man. But when he prayed, the quiet church and the peaceful candle drew his suffering out of him —

JESÚS: Madre María, ruega por nosotros —

NARRATOR ONE: He spilled his whispers out to the other Jesús, the man for whom he was named.

JESÚS: Jesús, allá en los cielos, haz el favor de cuidar el alma de mi zipote Juancito, que seguramente está volando a tu lado. Y gracias por todo lo que me has dado en este mundo.

JESÚS: Jesús now realized that he could not make enough money selling flowers to feed his family. So one day he told his wife —

JESÚS: Hey, Concepcíon. I'll be back in a couple of weeks with some money. I'm going down below; El Exigente's gonna give me a job. (JESÚS *goes down to the fields.*) Exigente!

FOREMAN: Eh?

JESÚS: Jesús!

FOREMAN: Right. You need a job, Man?

JESÚS: Claro.

FOREMAN: Over there.

JESÚS: Gracias.

NARRATOR TWO: So they put Jesús to work (*as* JESÚS *mimes the tasks*), cutting cane in the hot sun. Loading the one-hundred pound hands of bananas on to the truck. Hard work for an old man, getting older. But Jesús didn't complain.

(FOREMAN *returns, placing small amounts of money into imaginary hands. He pays* JESÚS; *starts to exit.*)

JESÚS (*looking in disbelief at his small pay*): No más?

FOREMAN: No más.

NARRATOR ONE: (*as* JESÚS *shrugs off disappointment and starts home*): Maybe then things might have reached a kind of balance again; Jesús had some cash, but one night after a week or two away, he went home —

JESÚS: Concepción! Conchita, I'm home.

NARRATOR ONE: His wife had died in childbirth, and the baby died with her.

NARRATOR TWO: Jesús hadn't known it, but she had been giving all the portions of food meant for her to her children, so they could grow strong. She and the baby inside her were expendable; they'd died of starvation. This is not an unusual event in a country like El Salvador, where seven out of ten children are starving.

Jesús took one of the pesos he'd earned down below; he went to the church and prayed for the salvation of his wife's soul.

JESÚS (*whispering prayer, lighting second candle*): Padre nuestro que estás en los cielos. . . . Jesucristo, haz el favor de cuidar el alma de mi esposa Concepción, que seguramente esta volando a tu lado, que voy a extrañarla mucho. . . .

(NARRATOR ONE *preparing for* MANUEL *role enters partially, quietly playing guitar. The music is a celestial response to* JESÚS's *reverie.*)

NARRATOR TWO: That was the first time that Jesús heard sounds in the old stone church. He seemed to hear a voice that said to him, (*changing to a deeper voice*): "Jesús. Presente. I am with you. Estoy aquí. I am here."

(JESÚS *mimes hearing the voice, feeling its strength enter him. With guitar music under, he mimes composite movements of his work: plow, hoe, dibble, cut flowers, cane, load fruit.*)

NARRATOR ONE: Jesús could not speak his sorrow to the world. He could do nothing but work harder, losing himself in his labor, dawn to dusk, coming home at night exhausted. Manuel, his friend with the guitar, came round one night. He was home from the University. He'd heard about Concepción.

MANUEL (*plucking a few notes on guitar*): Compa —

(JESÚS *looks at him, nods, says nothing.*)

MANUEL: Buenas tardes, Jesús. (*To* JESÚS's *imagined daughter*): Hola, Marta. (*To them both*): I'm sorry about Concepción.

JESÚS: Gracias.

MANUEL (*after painful silence, making conversation*): How's the corn coming, Man? (JESÚS *gestures "so high" weakly with one hand.*) I don't know how you do it, Jesús. You must be the best farmer in the village. How you grow that beautiful corn in your rockpile up there.

JESÚS: Rockpile! Hombre, that's my land. Doscientos —

MANUEL: I know, I know; two hundred years. Your father's father's father. And it's a great view up there. But you *could* have a piece of ground down below. Long straight furrows. Deep soil. Water. Like your ancestors had. Of course, that was before the coffee growers took it all away. 1875, 1880. They took everything, Man. 'Course, that was long before your time —

JESÚS: Sí.

MANUEL: Now, *during* your time the peasants tried to get some of it back. Till 1932, of course; the government sent out the soldiers and they massacred 30,000 campesinos in a couple of weeks; what's that, about two thousand a day? Men, women, children: after that, the silence —

JESÚS: Manuel —

MANUEL: What?

JESÚS: That was my mother and father.

MANUEL: Ay! I'm sorry, Jesús. I don't know what gets into me. I start

13

talkin' about corn and I end up with a massacre. Maybe I better play you a song. (*He plays.*)

JESÚS: Wait: why do you always talk about these things? How do you know all this?

MANUEL: School, Man. I've been to school. Studied real hard. And all I got, look: (*pulling out empty pocket*): a license to practice poverty! Oh, that's not all. I also got a Masters in Malnutrition. (*poking JESÚS in stomach*): Just like you! (*He plays guitar again.*) Look, Man, the sun is shining. We're gonna get by.

NARRATOR TWO: Well, Jesús knew that he had to get by. He had no choice. So he put his mind to it, and he thought of something else, now, that he could do with the flowers he picked on the mountain. Some of them he wouldn't sell right away. He'd take them home and hang them on the rafters of his house to dry. When they were dry he'd weave them into sculptures infinitely fine, with his rough hands, of children, oxcarts, animals, saints, La Virgen de las Flores, Nuestro Señor del Petate — and these little flower sculptures by Jesús brought a pretty good price at the marketplace on Sundays, when the families came out to buy. . . . (*Here, while JESÚS works, the continuing guitar indicates passing time, though the two men do not move about.*)

MANUEL (*looking over at MARTA*): Jesús, Marta is so beautiful.

JESÚS: Sí.

MANUEL: She looks just like Concepción. I'll bet she can cook like her, too.

JESÚS: Sí, Concepción taught her everything —

MANUEL: She'll make a wonderful wife for a man someday —

(JESÚS, *shocked, looks at* MANUEL.)

MANUEL: I mean, she's too beautiful for this village, Man. I could take her away with me to Mexico City. . . . No, Acapulco! Then we send for you —

JESÚS (*angry*): No comprendes! You don't understand. Since Concepción died, Marta is everything to us. We need her. *We* love her. She makes the best tortillas in town. She washes the clothes so white on the stones of the waterfall. We couldn't do without her!

MANUEL: Okay, okay: I'm just telling you; guard her close. 'Cause she might turn up missing one night.

JESÚS: Missing?

MANUEL: Yes. I'm going to ride by on my white horse, and carry her off to Miami Beach!

JESÚS: Ay! (*He swats* MANUEL *with the broom*) Fuera! (*Exit* MANUEL.)

NARRATOR TWO: So you see, these two men had a lot of ideas about what Marta was going to do with her life. That's the way some men are. But Marta had ideas of her own: she wanted to do something completely different. Meanwhile, she had begun to train her sister, María, to take over the household tasks, and one night she came to her father and said, "Papacito, ya me voy," "Papa, I'm going away, if you please—" but not to get married, not even to a good man like Manuel. Marta wanted to go to a town nearby, to work there with the Catholic nuns who had just come in to that part of the country. They had come to distribute food, to teach people how to read, and to help some of the poor people to sit down with each other, to talk about their problems. They had come from places like Oklahoma, Detroit, Nueva Jersey, even Brooklyn, New York City. They had white skin and blue eyes and short hair; they wore pants just like men — Marta was very impressed by them. She wanted to go help, too, and Jesús was proud to think of Marta going off to help people even poorer than they were. Of course he gave his consent.

(*While* JESÚS *bids good-bye to* MARTA, *then waves her out of sight*):

Now, had Jesús known what was going to happen to her, he surely would not have given his permission for her to go. How was he to know that to do the kind of work the nuns were doing in that country at that time was to cross the will of the government, was to risk death? And one night soon after, Marta and three of her friends were crammed into a Volkswagen bug with their boxes of bread. They had been at a meeting of landless farmers. It was very dark; they were riding along a bumpy road by a cliff. Up ahead, there was a boulder in the road where it shouldn't have been. They stopped the car; they all got out to see if they could move it — instantly, some government soldiers sprang from behind the rock! Some others scurried down the cliff: it was an ambush!

There were witnesses hiding in the shadows — they heard the major holler to his soldiers, "Men, use the women as you wish!" They saw Marta and her three friends raped, then killed like animals. Marta was only sixteen years old. They saw the flaming wreck of the Volkswagen rolled over the cliff. They saw the soldiers drag the bodies of the women away, dump them down a 150-foot well and throw a stick of dynamite after to bury the evidence.

Jesús heard that his daughter was missing. Desaparecida. For two days he could do nothing.

JESÚS: Que Marta tiene nada mas que diez y seis años! Sixteen years old!

NARRATOR TWO: — he couldn't work or eat or sleep. For two days. Finally he went to look for information. To San Salvador. This time no flowers on his back. He went to the office of the Comandante, but that Comandante must have been a very busy man: he made Jesús wait for seven hours in the outer room, while he went about his day's work. (*During this speech,* COMANDANTE *appears, sits on left stool, talks on phone.* JESÚS *descends, holding* MARTA's *picture, waits.*)

JESÚS (*bursting in at last*): Hábla-me, mi Coronel. Speak with me.

COMANDANTE (*into phone*): Sí, sí mas tarde. Ten-four. (*To* JESÚS): Díga-me.

JESÚS: This is the picture of my daughter Marta. She's missing for two days. They said you have information —

COMANDANTE (*showing* JESÚS *papers*): Hombre, tengo pruebas aquí — these are captured documents, Man —

(JESÚS *gestures he cannot read.*)

COMANDANTE: They prove that those nuns your daughter was working for are Communists. Now you know how the people of this country hate Communists. I can't be responsible for what my soldiers might do when they catch a carload of commies trying to run a roadblock. Hey, it's been a tough day, old man. I'm tired. You're tired. I gotta go to an important meeting. Go home; get some sleep; you'll feel better in the morning —

JESÚS (*holding out hand, almost inaudible*): Help me —

COMANDANTE (*misunderstanding, hands* JESÚS *a coin*): Here, go get yourself a drink. Make you feel better.

(JESÚS *stares at the coin a long time, finally gives it back.*)

COMANDANTE: Pues, jodete. (Ho·de·te.)

(JESÚS *moves away slowly;* COMANDANTE *mimes getting into car, driving off.*)

NARRATOR TWO: So the Comandante left Jesús there. He drove across town to his apartment in the suburbs. (*COMANDANTE screeches to stop; enters house, whistles to his maid, offstage.*) He called for a beer.

COMANDANTE: Teresa! Cerveza!

NARRATOR TWO: The Comandante loved it in the can.

(*Mime in this scene:* COMANDANTE *flirting with imaginary maid, shaking, popping, spraying, drinking illusory beer can. Responding to maid's temper, watching TV.*)

NARRATOR TWO: He settled back in his plastic chaise lounge, and turned on the TV:

TELEVISION (*one actor framing head with forearms*): Gracias, Señoras y Señores, esto fué Starsky and Hutch. Nuestro programa se presentó hoy por COCA-COLA: "Disfrute la chispa de la vida!" Y por Walt Dees-ney World; viaje al mundo asombroso de Deesney! Y por Braneef International — viaje a la alegría con Braneef. Y por las siguientes grandes empresas multinacionales de Drogas, Smeeth Klein, Lily, Squeeb, and Merk, that sell you in San Salvador tetracycline and the other drugs you so desperately need for ten, twenty, thirty, times what they cost the folks back in the states! Y ahora, vamos a ver: MISION IMPOSIBLE! (*Mimes, with sound effects, random TV violence: sirens, cops, cars, doors slamming, gunshots, screams, telephones, knives, rape, running, fists, sirens; violence spills out of TV screen, attacking COMANDANTE; he laughs and turns it off: quick electronic dissolve.*)

COMANDANTE: I got it made down here, Man. All I gotta do is tell Uncle Sam I'm down here fighting Communists. He sends me anything I ask: weapons, tanks, helicopters, (*patting pocket*), lunch money, good beer —heh! People say, someday he's gonna find out. Don't you believe it! (*Absent-mindedly shakes already-opened fresh beer can. It spills on his shirt.*) Ay, mierda!

(END ACT ONE)

18

ACT TWO

NARRATOR TWO (*as* JESÚS *slowly mounts the stage*): Jesús aged ten years that night. It took him till the sun was high the next day, to walk back up to San Pedro el Pacífico. He didn't know whether Marta was alive or dead —

(JESÚS *pauses at church as if deciding; enters, lights third candle, prays.*)

JESÚS: Padre nuestro, yo no sé si está viva o muerta mi hija Marta; haz el favor de cuidar su alma — gracias por todo. . . .

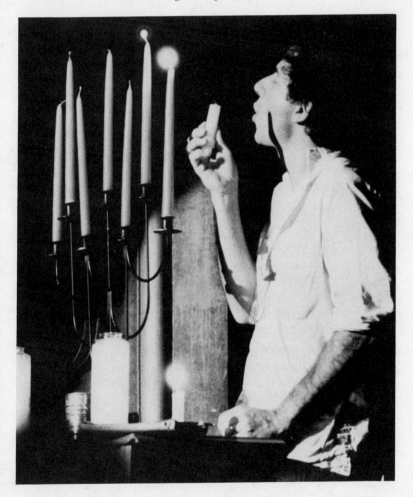

NARRATOR TWO: He waited to hear the voices, but there were none. (*Enter* RAUL, *brief tableau then action of plowing.*) Jesús had a son, Raul. He was strong and quiet just like his father. He had claimed a piece of land; he hoped to get married soon. (NARRATOR TWO *walks over to* RAUL's *side.*) When he found out —

NARRATOR TWO (*speaking as a* NEIGHBOR): Your sister's missing!

RAUL: Marta?

NARRATOR/NEIGHBOR: Sí! Hace dos noches.

RAUL: Dónde?

NARRATOR/NEIGHBOR: En la carretera a Usulután! (*pointing off stageright*

NARRATOR TWO: He went to get information. (RAUL *enters audience, running.*) He went down the road he knew she'd been traveling.

RAUL: Have you seen my sister? (*To individuals in audience*): Her name is Marta. She was with the nuns.

NARRATOR TWO: He went to the last town where she'd been seen alive. No one would talk to him —

RAUL: I am Raul, Jesús's son. You know me. Their car went by your house —

NARRATOR TWO: They were all too afraid.

RAUL: Where is she? Why won't you talk to me? Was it the Death Squads? Orden? Mano Blanco? Tell me —

NARRATOR TWO: He asked too many questions; he asked the wrong people. The Security Police came.

RAUL (*facing imaginary troopers*): I am looking for my sister. My name is Raul. From San Pedro. No, I don't have any pa- (*falling as if struck in stomach*): Get your hands off me! I'm looking for my sister! I haven't done any- (*He is dragged off stage*): Somebody help me! Tell them you know me!

NARRATOR TWO: For the first time in Jesús's life, a member of his family was cast down into prison. There he stayed for months, locked in a basement somewhere. Now Jesús had a lot more work to do. Two plots of ground. His son would need food when he came home.

And as he worked in the hot sun, watering the crops with his tears, he found himself praying for Raul to be sent home; he knew he was alive.

JESÚS (*resting from the plow and hoe*): Yo lo necesito aquí, para que me ayude con la milpa. Es mucho trabajo para un hombre solo, viejo como yo. Oyes? Are you listening?

NARRATOR TWO: But always it seemed to him that there was nobody listening. No one to hear the cry of the poor. At last one night he went to the church —

(*As* JESÚS *enters church stage right,* RAUL *in silence, in dim light where possible, is heaved in, stage left. He comes to rest against left-hand stool. His shirt is bloodied and his hands appear tied behind his back.*)

JESÚS (*in church, wearily lighting fourth candle*): Padre nuestro —

NARRATOR TWO: He promised he would never ask another favor.

JESÚS: Yo te juro que no te voy a pedir ni una cosita mas. Devuélveme Raul.

NARRATOR TWO: Maybe a miracle happened that night; maybe some- one did hear. Or perhaps, just by chance, a warden in the prison flipped a coin and said, "this one will go free," because the next day an unusual event for El Salvador took place:

(PRISON GUARD *enters, either another actor, or quick role change — just in voice — by* NARRATOR TWO.)

PRISON GUARD (*clapping hands explosively*): Levanta-te! Wake up! (*He mimes the drawing of a sheath-knife.* RAUL *backs away in terror.* GUARD *swings knife quickly, cuts the string around* RAUL's *thumbs.*) Puedes partir.

(RAUL *backs away, rubbing thumbs.*)

PRISON GUARD: Ora-le! (*Pushing him toward imaginary door, then stopping him suddenly.*) No digas nada de lo que pasó aquí! (*Say nothing about what happened here.*)

RAUL (*whispering*): Sí.

PRISON GUARD: Y la proxima vez que vengas — (*And the next time you come.*) (GUARD *makes quick knife motion across* RAUL's *neck*). Ahora —

RAUL (*whispering*): Sí.

PRISON GUARD (*slapping* RAUL *on backside*): Buena suerte. (*Exit both.*)

NARRATOR TWO (*as* JESÚS *sits on his stool*): Raul was pale now, and tired; he walked with a limp. But most of the scars were inside him. Jesús was sitting on his stone bench under the pomegranate tree, watching the end of another afternoon on the ridges and valleys before him —

RAUL (*entering from audience*): Papá.

JESÚS: Hijo! (*They embrace,* JESÚS *waving in gratitude to the sky.*)

21

RAUL (*pulling away, making for the house*): Marta!

JESÚS (*to himself*): No.

RAUL: Marta?

JESÚS (*to* RAUL): No. Marta no.

RAUL: Eh?

JESÚS: Nunca vino.

RAUL: Eh?

JESÚS: Se desapareció. She never came back.

RAUL (*after long pause, going to the house again*): María!

JESÚS: Sí (*Nodding quietly, as if understanding what is happening*): María, si. María sí está.

NARRATOR TWO: Raul found his second sister, María. They talked together quietly, packed a bag, and went off, together, to join the rebels arming and fighting now in the mountains to the north —

(*Appropriate place here for music: instrumental, Central American, quiet, determined, under the next three speeches.*)

RAUL: Hasta la vista, Papá. (RAUL *and* JESÚS *embrace.*)

JESÚS: Buena suerte, Hijo. María: vaya con Dios. (*They embrace.*)

NARRATOR TWO (*as* RAUL — *and* MARIA, *if she is portrayed* — *act out the journey and the training*): They didn't want to have to do it. They would much rather have stayed at home, working in the field, the house, raising a family, going to school. They didn't want to have to do it. But just as before them, in Cuba, in Nicaragua, brother and sister found their difficult way to the mountain camps of the rebels.

They didn't want to have to do it. They were people exactly like you (*to the audience*), many of them about your age. They had dreams, ambitions. But now they had seen their friends, their parents, their children, cut apart by machetes by government soldiers or death squads right in front of their eyes. They had no choice; they lived in a land ruled by institutional terror — they went off to learn how to defend themselves, how to survive in the forest, they already knew how to live on almost nothing. And meanwhile, far away in Washington, D.C., a high administration official was holding a press briefing:

(*Enter* U.S. GOVERNMENT SPOKESMAN, *in suit and tie. He mimes holding attaché case or sheaf of papers. He speaks, a flat voice, through a microphone.*)

SPOKESMAN: Good afternoon. We now have overwhelming and irrefutable evidence that Salvadoran guerillas are passing in and out of Nicaragua for advanced training in sabotage and other terrorist tactics. Every day the leftist guerillas commit new atrocities against their fellow countrymen. May I have the first slide, please?

(JESÚS *enters, snaps into still pose of plowing.*)

SPOKESMAN: This slide shows a Communist rebel attacking our photographer, who barely escaped with the picture. Next:

(JESÚS *snaps into still pose of hoe-ing.*)

SPOKESMAN: Notice here this guerilla is wearing a Cuban-style shirt. He's also armed with a Soviet-built weapon.

(JESÚS *snaps into pose of planting with dibble stick.*)

SPOKESMAN: This slide shows a subversive attacking an innocent baby. The baby is just below the frame of the picture. Next, please.

(JESÚS *snaps into flower-selling pose.*)

SPOKESMAN: Here we see a poor old campesino forced to sell flowers in the marketplace to earn protection money for his terrorist bosses. Just look at that. Thank you. (JESÚS *exits.*) In conclusion, there is no doubt at all that this is Fidel Castro up to his old tricks. Cuba has embarked upon a systematic campaign, orchestrated in Moscow, to destabilize legitimate governments in Colombia, Honduras, Nicaragua, El Salvador, Jamaica, Guatemala, and El, El, uh, elsewhere. And we do have to make sure that we don't allow on the mainland of the United States a bastion of Communism, a foothold. That would make the defense of the United States infinitely more difficult. And I am sure the American public will support whatever is prudently necessary in the way of U.S. aid — provided they think we mean what we mean. (*Pause to check notes.*) And what we mean is that this time we are going to succeed, and not flounder as we did in Vietnam. This time we are going to win. We will not let another free and democratic government go down the drain. Good afternoon. Thank you very much. No, I cannot speak about our sources. Thank you. Good afternoon.

NARRATOR TWO (*as* JESÚS *enters sweeping his front yard, and shaking his head, "no," at two imaginary passers-by*): People began to come to Jesús's door now to say, "Hey, Old Man, where's your son; we heard he was out of jail." Jesús said nothing. He never had talked much, and now it grew harder to know whom to trust. He still worked his land, picked the flowers, hiked to the capital. But there was a new feeling in the land: tension, violence much more in the open now. There were three or four hundred people per week now, gone: some became refugees, but most were missing or dead. There were soldiers everywhere, wearing new uniforms, driving new four-wheel drive trucks. You never knew when a squadron might appear, searching the homes in your village, dragging your neighbors away —

Soldiers and security police stood outside of churches, watching who came to the services. At night they took off their uniforms; they became the death squads. They followed the movements of priests and nuns, listened to what they preached and taught. The stories grew worse now: five hundred school teachers killed, shot in their class-rooms, priests and health care workers killed while making their rounds.

And still there were those who said, "We don't know who's doing all this killing. The soldiers are our friends; we should invite them into our town. They're going to help us with the land reform. La Reforma Agraria, Phase One. The wealthy families are going to give up one per-cent of their land, so that four million of us can grow our plots of corn. The government has even declared a State of siege to make it happen; that's why the soldiers are here.

Land Reform! Everyone was talking about it. They said it was made up in the great universities of the United States, and they said it was tried out so successfully in South Vietnam!

(*Enter* SALVADORAN OFFICER, *wearing camouflage cap, mirror sun glasses, black gloves; he mimes driving a large truck. His clenched fist is the microphone of a static-filled truck-roof-mounted public address system.*)

OFFICER: Atención! Atención! Atención: campesinos, gather round! (*He opens door, swings down from truck, slams door.*) (*Shouting now*): Campesinos, gather round, (*to the audience*): anda-le! Let's go — all right! (*Less loud*): The boys in the truck and I have come to help you out. Don't worry about the rifles; they're here to protect you. (*Now he addresses individual audience members as villagers.*) Okay: we understand that some of you in this village have lost your land, no? You? And you? Correcto? Lost your land, eh? What's that — you say you never had any — okay, we understand, it's a bad business. But not to worry. We got a good government now, and this government is institut-ing what is to be called "The Land Reform." Phase One. What this means is that everybody is gonna have a nice piece of land. The older people, young people, (*to a hairy member of the audience*): even heepies like you. Ha! All right. In order to make sure that it's done fair and square, we have to take a tour around and look at the land situa-tion. And for that purpose I'd like now for the leaders of this village please to step forward. Por favor. (*No one comes forward; he waits.*) I said, I'd like the leaders of the village to step forward, gracias. (*He

waits. Then, more seriously): Who are the leaders of this village?
(*Waits.*) You want this land reform?

You: (*to a man*): you're wearing glasses; are you the leader of this village? No? Well, who is? (*To a woman*): Sweetheart, (*playing with her hair*), you tell me who the leader is, and I'll give you the nicest piece of land, hmm? Keep my soldiers away from you, huh?

All right! (*To* JESÚS): Old Man, are you the leader of this village?

JESÚS: No.

OFFICER: What is this, you don't have any leaders?

JESÚS: Eso.

OFFICER (*laughing loud and long*): Ha, hey Boys, heh, we are in a leaderless village! Si! (*To the audience again, menacing*): That's all right. No problem. So you don't have any leaders — tomorrow you will have two. 'Cause tonight you hold an election — you like elections, don't you, eh — you choose two leaders, tomorrow we come back, we talk with them, we check out the land situation. Hasta mañana! (*He drives away.*)

NARRATOR TWO: That was the happiest night of Jesús's life. Everyone in the town got together in the stone church and held that election.

25

Jesús's second son, Ricardo, the school teacher, was one of the two people chosen land reform leaders of San Pedro el Pacífico. Jesús was so proud. He and his son sat up all night, drinking the hot corn drink, talking about the terrible way things had been, and about the land reform, and about the way that things were going to change now —

OFFICER (*arriving again in truck, announcing as before*): Atención! Atención! Everybody gather round! Campesinos! Buenos días; it's a beautiful day, no? All right: let's get to work on this land reform. (*While he is speaking* JESÚS *is beckoning to his imaginary son to come.*) You had your election? Good: who are your leaders?

JESÚS: Aquí. (*His hand is raised as if guiding his son's back.*)

OFFICER: Who's this?

JESÚS: It's my son, Ricardo. He's the school teacher.

OFFICER: A smart boy, eh?

JESÚS: Sí, muy listo.

OFFICER: Bueno, Ricardo, step to the back of the truck. (*Then, looking toward a second imaginary figure*): Who's this? Good, good. Boys, give them a hand up. All right. Watch your step. Now everybody remember, the land reform is for you, all of you. You will not get the title to the land now; that will come later. We got a good government now. (*Getting back into the truck cab*): So, if we stick together, we shall overcome!

JESÚS: Ricardo, aquí te espero! (*He reaches up to squeeze son's hand.*)

OFFICER: Hasta la vista! (*He drives away.*)

JESÚS: Sí, aquí no más! (*Waving*): Hasta pronto. (*Waving his hat now, back to the audience*): Aquí te espero! (*To the audience*): That's my son! (*He turns away again, waving hat, turns back to the audience, nervously smiling.*)

NARRATOR TWO (*Sitting on edge of stage carefully, or on left stool brought forward. He chooses his words carefully.*): You know, Jesús never saw his son again. Nobody knows where those two bodies lie. But I can tell you this: those two people in the truck were tortured. Tortured to death — by men who don't do it to get information. They don't even do it like in the good old days: for revenge. They torture for one reason, and that is: to keep people like you and me in constant terror, so we won't try to do anything. It almost works! Sometimes they use simple instruments, like cigarettes, plastic bags, pins. Sometimes they use more intricate machines. The instructions are in English.

They're manufactured in the United States of America, and sold in Latin America for a profit, or sent there as a gift. The United States is, or has been a major exporter of torture technology and practice. It's hard to prove this. Some people say: it's not in the budget anymore; the Congress won't allow it. It doesn't matter . . . Jesús's son was tortured. His cries in the night were dimly heard by people like us, waiting outside the building for a bit of news, a word, the whereabouts of a friend, a father, a wife, a teacher, a son. But no word ever came. Desaparecidos. They had disappeared. Officially. Forever.

(JESÚS *goes to the church. He lights a candle; he begins to form a prayer, but stands speechless in candle-light.*)

NARRATOR TWO: Jesús stood in the plaza. For the first time, he felt himself the only man alive in San Pedro el Pacífico. So this was what a town was like, when people disappeared. He went up to his land. He felt the urge to plow, to plant, for no one. He didn't know why: just force of habit, the only life he knew —

(JESÚS *trying to plow, to hoe, lacking the energy of completion. Victor Jara music, "El Arado," under.* MANUEL *enters, carrying his guitar and a duffel, breathless, calling* JESÚS *down.*)

MANUEL: Jesús! Hombre! There you are! I'm home —

JESÚS (*nodding, inaudibly*): From school, sí —

MANUEL: No, not from school, man. I quit school. I've been to the new El Salvador. I've joined a comunidad de base, a base community: guess what I'm doing? (JESÚS *is not responding to* MANUEL's *enthusiasm.*) I'm teaching people to read and write. Yes! Hey, I've seen María —

JESÚS: María!

MANUEL: And Raul. They're okay. Raul is fighting; María, she's working in a hospital. They got a little clinic up there — some of the sick people are seeing a doctor for the first time in their lives. Hey, I've got something for you. (*He searches in duffel, pulls out a small poster of Archbishop Romero.*) On my way back from the north, I stopped in San Salvador. I heard Monseñor speak at his church. Look. You know him?

JESÚS (*shaking head*): No.

MANUEL (*spelling out the name on poster*): Arch-bishop Os-car Ro-me-ro. You see? He is giving homilies every Sunday. You know what he said? He said the rich people in Salvador are causing all the evil. They'll do anything to *us* to make a bigger profit.

JESÚS: Can I have this?

MANUEL: Sure, put it up on the wall — when's the last time you heard a priest talk like that? (JESÚS *hangs the picture.*) He is going way out on a limb, and people are getting together out there with him. (JESÚS *stares at the picture.*) You want to hear him speak? Look.

JESÚS: Eh?

MANUEL (*searching duffel*): Look, I brought you a radio. Here: On, Off, Volume. (*He turns it on; a few seconds of bolero-type music are heard.*) You listen on Sunday; you'll hear Monseñor speak.

JESÚS: Gracias.

MANUEL: I've got to get going. Wait, something else: would you take care of my guitar for me? The way I'm traveling, I'm afraid it'll get broken. Here, learn a song for me —

JESÚS: No puedo —

MANUEL: I mean it. You teach it to me when I come back.

JESÚS (*as if trying to hold Manuel back from leaving*): You come back soon and get it.

MANUEL (*Seeing* JESÚS *clearly*): Hey, I should have asked you before: you want to come with me?

JESÚS: No, I have to wait for Ricardo.

MANUEL (*after pause*): All right. Hey, Jesús, stay out of trouble. You don't know anything, right? Nada. Lay low.

JESÚS: Sí.

MANUEL: Take care of the guitar. Don't get it wet.

JESÚS: No.

MANUEL: Don't keep her out too late.

JESÚS: No.

MANUEL: At night put her under your bed. (*He starts to leave.*)

JESÚS: Under the bed.

MANUEL (*Farther off*): Sí.

JESÚS: Manuel!

MANUEL (*from a distance*): Eh?

JESÚS: I don't have a bed.

MANUEL: Ay! Good-bye, Jesús.

NARRATOR TWO (*as* JESÚS *puts guitar in house*): That fall Jesús went down below as he always did: to find El Exigente, to see about having his job back.

JESÚS: Exigente!

FOREMAN: Hombre, que querés?

JESÚS: Jesús. Estoy aquí de nuevo.

FOREMAN: You want your old job, Jesús?

JESÚS: Claro.

FOREMAN: Well, Old Man, I can't use you any more.

JESÚS: Cómo?

FOREMAN: You're getting too old.

JESÚS (*making a muscle*): Pero sigo fuerte.

FOREMAN: I know. You're a good worker, Jesús. Look: you see that machine over there? That machine does the job of twenty men, all night long, under the lights, and it doesn't complain like people do. So I gotta go, Man. Business is business.

JESÚS (*tipping hat*): Gracias.

FOREMAN: Look, you need money? Tell your kids to go down to San Salvador. They can get a job in a factory. (*He leaves.*)

JESÚS: I can work all night. I don't complain. (*Looking at a member of the audience, making a muscle*): Sigo fuerte, no? (*I'm still strong.*)

NARRATOR ONE (*as* JESÚS *plods home*): So the old man made the nine-mile hike back to his village, back to San Pedro el Pacifico. He climbed straight past his house, up to his plot of ground, his only joy now — he wanted to see the ripening corn, to feel the sun-warmed soil, to belong again among his ancestors — (JESÚS *approaches his land, is stopped by something invisible*): But when he got there, he couldn't get in!

JESÚS: Alambre!

NARRATOR ONE: There was barbed wire encircling the entire piece of ground.

JESÚS (*pulling, getting cut*): Hey!

NARRATOR ONE: He had no tools; he couldn't cut it down. He looked inside; there were cattle —

JESÚS: Vacas!

NARRATOR ONE: The cattle were trampling his corn, chewing the ears — Jesús went wild —

JESÚS (*on his knees, throwing stones*): Saca-te! Es maíz! Get out! Es mi pedacito de terreno! That's my land!

NARRATOR ONE: He ran down to the village, house to house. What has happened to my land? No one would talk to him. They were all too afraid. Finally in a neighboring village someone pointed him toward the hacienda. A rich man came out. He waved a piece of paper in Jesús's face. The land was his now, after two hundred years. The title to that land had cost him one bottle of scotch whiskey.

(JESÚS *stands alone, center stage, hat almost crushed in his hands. The perpetual smile on his face is twisted now. He may or may not speak*):

JESÚS: Doscientos años. Two hundred years.

NARRATOR ONE: Jesús all alone now. No wife, no job, no kids, no land. Still the old man doesn't complain. He is a quiet man, meeting his fate like a piece of ground, accepting what the farmer does to it. For two days he sits on his bench, under the pomegranate tree, not eating or sleeping, looking for signs of hope, watching: the butterfly by day, the star by night. . . . Some of his neighbors come by; they whisper to him, when they're sure no one is there from the security forces, or the death squads, like ORDEN or Mano Blanco. They tell him, almost everyone has suffered as Jesús has. Whole towns have been destroyed by the government troops; they burn them to the ground; they bulldoze the winter storage of corn and beans. There's nothing to come back to. Survivors take off to the mountains of the north, fleeing for their lives. Some make it to refugee camps, some go with the rebels, and some, like Maria and Manuel, join "comunidades de base," base camps, new communities, where they work for peace. Old people learn to read; the young have food and medical care. They talk about Nicaragua, about the Gospel, about this or that massacre that opened their eyes, about the new El Salvador. And in their work, they're helped by the rebels, and by country priests and school teachers — some of the ones who haven't been killed.

NARRATOR TWO: Jesús learned a lot in those days. He lived alone; he was a good listener. People knew he could keep a secret; they came and spilled their stories out to him, just as he, in the church, told his truth to the man for whom he was named. The village compressed; it was like a family now, brought together by its suffering. And Jesús was the old keeper of its stories.

Now Jesús had a radio, too — sometimes on a Sunday night the people gathered round it, listening to the Archbishop. They heard him say, "My brothers and sisters, siempre hay esperanza; there is always hope. They may kill us all — he always said *us* — but the cry of the people will go on and on."

Monseñor had started out as a conservative priest. He had been chosen Archbishop because the church thought he'd be a safe candidate; he wouldn't be outspoken. For a while that prediction held. He traveled the country; he spoke to the people most poor and suffering. But what he learned he didn't speak of. Till the day his favorite priest was murdered by the death squads: Rutilio Grande: un hombre sin pecado, they called him: a man without sin. On that day Romero was converted. He started to speak out about what the poor had told him. His voice became the loudest all over the world, telling the atrocities that the government of El Salvador was doing to its own people. His words flew to the mountain villages, where Jesús and people like him listened. It was a country full of transistor radios, and the Archbishop had his own station, YSAX, "La Voz Panamericana," broadcasting every day despite the slander, harassment, death threats. Once even, Monseñor came to San Pedro el Pacífico —

ROMERO (*entering from offstage, or through audience*): Brothers and sisters, come out of your houses. Gather round, let us talk together; there is no one here from the army. Dios te bendiga. (*To members of the audience*): God bless you. Come out, come out.

JESÚS (*looking at his picture*): Monseñor!

ROMERO: What is your name?

JESÚS (*falling to his knees, taking* ROMERO's *hand*): Jesús.

ROMERO: Ah, Jesús. Tell me about your life. Have you lost your land?

JESÚS (*pointing*): Estaba allí.

ROMERO: Your children —

JESÚS: Casi todos.

ROMERO: Your neighbors have lost children?

JESÚS: Speak with them —

ROMERO (*to the audience*): Ah, your brother has been shot by the security forces? Your daughter is malnourished. They have taken your land. (*Speaking out to all now*): My brothers and sisters, you may well ask, "What is to be done?" I answer, the hope that the church fosters is a call to the poor, to you, to the vast majority, that you begin to take responsibility for your own future, that you organize. It is the poor who are forcing *us* to understand what is really taking place here in El Salvador.

One who is committed to the poor must suffer the same fate as the poor. And in El Salvador we know what the fate of the poor signifies:

to be found missing, to be held captive, to be tortured, to turn up somewhere on a roadside, a corpse. When a dictatorship has so attacked human rights, when it becomes unbearable, all channels of dialogue are cut off, then the church may speak of your legitimate right to armed insurrection. Let us pray together.

(*Pause.* ROMERO *and* JESÚS *pray silently.*)

ROMERO: May God have mercy on our souls. Amen. (*To* JESÚS): Peace be with you, Jesús.

JESÚS: And also with you, Monseñor. (*He exits.*)

ROMERO: Ahh. They have threatened my life so many times. If they should kill me I will rise again in the Salvadoran people, and I don't say that boastingly, but as humbly as I can. Martyrdom is a grace of God I do not feel worthy of, but if God should accept the sacrifice of my body, then my hope is that my blood will be as a seed of liberty, and a sign that our hopes will soon become a reality. May God be with you all.

NARRATOR TWO (*as* ROMERO *leaves*): Revolutionary words for an archbishop to say. Just think: for four hundred years the Catholic Church had been telling the poor people of El Salvador, we know how terrible things are for you on earth. But just wait; in heaven you'll be fine. And now for a few years some of the church workers, country priests and nuns, lay helpers like Marta, had gone to stand with the poor, to help them get back some of what they had lost. But Monseñor Romero was the first priest to say for all to hear, "I forgive you; the church must forgive you, for whatever *you may have to do.*" Jesús found strength in that meeting and those words, to live day by day, picking his flowers and preparing his simple meals, and dwelling deeply within his hope, that someday, quizás mañana, maybe tomorrow, things would change.

Well, things did change. They only got worse. Hundreds more innocent people died. Monseñor asked himself, what can I do? He decided to write a letter to the President of the United States: "Dear Mr. President, please stop sending the weapons and ammunition down to El Salvador. The government is only using them to kill its own people. You are a Christian, Mr. President; I know you would not want to be responsible for crushing the just hopes of the Salvadoran people."

I guess the President didn't read his mail, because the weapons, the ammunition, kept coming. So many more people died: Monseñor asked himself, what more can I do? He decided to speak to the soldiers of the army; he'd never tried that before. He addressed them from his pulpit in San Salvador; the words he said were broadcast all over the country; people like you, like us, we got together around the radios —

(NARRATOR TWO *holds up Jesús's radio, looks round as if gathering people to listen, turns it on, volume high*):

ROMERO'S VOICE ON RADIO: Yo quisiera hacer un llamamento de manera especial . . .

NARRATOR TWO: I want to make a special call —

VOICE: A los hombres del ejército . . .

NARRATOR TWO: To the men of the army —

VOICE: Y en concreto, a las bases de la guardia nacional, de la policía . . .

NARRATOR TWO: And concretely, to the bases of the national guard and police.

VOICE: Hermanos:

NARRATOR TWO: Brothers:

VOICE: Son de nuestro mismo pueblo . . .

NARRATOR TWO: You come from the same people as we —

VOICE: Matan a sus mismos hermanos campesinos . . .

NARRATOR TWO: You are killing your brothers and sisters, the peasants —

VOICE: Y ante una orden de matar que dé un hombre . . .

NARRATOR TWO: And when faced with an order to kill, given by a man —

VOICE: Debe obedecer . . .

NARRATOR TWO: You should rather obey —

VOICE: La ley de Dios, que dice, No Matar!

NARRATOR TWO: The law of God: Thou Shalt Not Kill!

VOICE: Ningun soldado . . .

NARRATOR TWO: No soldier —

VOICE: Está obligado . . .

NARRATOR TWO: Is obligated —

VOICE: A obedecer una orden contra la ley de Dios.

NARRATOR TWO: To obey an order against God's law.

VOICE: Una ley immoral . . .

NARRATOR TWO: An immoral law —

VOICE: Nadie tiene que cumplirla.

NARRATOR TWO: Nobody has to obey!

VOICE: La iglesia no puede quedarse callada ante tanta abominación.

NARRATOR TWO: The church cannot keep quiet, faced with such abomination.

VOICE: En nombre de Dios, pues . . .

NARRATOR TWO: In the name of God, therefore —

VOICE: Y en nombre de este sufrido pueblo . . .

NARRATOR TWO: And in the name of this suffering people —

VOICE: Cuyos lamentos suben al cielo cada día mas tumultuosos . . .

NARRATOR TWO: Whose cries climb up to heaven, louder every day —

VOICE: Les suplico,

NARRATOR TWO: I urge you,

VOICE: Les ruego,

NARRATOR TWO: I beg you,

VOICE: Les ordeno, en nombre de Dios,

NARRATOR TWO: I order you, in the name of God,

VOICE: Cese la represión!

NARRATOR TWO: Stop the repression!

(MONSEÑOR'S *finale is drowned by applause on the radio;* NARRATOR TWO *waits, then turns the radio off, saying*):

NARRATOR TWO: Well, I guess the Archbishop must have gone too far. Because it was the *very next day* —

(*Enter a* BOY (or a GIRL), *running, breathless, the voice heard first from without*):

BOY: Has oído? Has oído las noticias? (*Arriving on stage*): Have you heard the news? (JESÚS *appears.*)

JESÚS: No —

BOY: Monseñor! Monseñor está muerto!

JESÚS: Muerto!

BOY: They have killed the Archbishop! Romero, Monseñor — they killed him right in the chapel of the hospital. It was a hit man; he sneaked in. Monseñor was holding the cup; he was saying the Mass. He shot him right in the chest, an exploding bullet; it has blown up his chest —

JESÚS: No puede ser —

BOY: He's dead! (*Starting away*): Monseñor está muerto! (*Pulling free from* JESÚS'S *grasp, running out through audience*): Mataron a Monseñor! Han oído las noticias!

(JESÚS *stands, back to audience, looking at the picture. As he turns*):

NARRATOR TWO: He was killed in a chapel, a room like this one. Witnesses were sitting there, just as you are. Everybody knew who was responsible, who had planned the deed, who had drawn lots to choose who would pull the trigger. But when the news broke in the United States of America, it came out twisted as it so often does: "No group has claimed responsibility; we don't know who committed this terrible deed; both sides could stand to profit; another victim of the escalating violence between Left and Right." But Jesús, simple man, up in San Pedro el Pacífico: he knew, and he understood. (JESÚS *walks toward the church.*) Which is not to say that he believed what he had heard. . . .

JESÚS (*at prayer, lighting a candle*): Padre nuestro que estás en los cielos —

NARRATOR TWO: In the church he lost all track of time. Long after everyone else had left, Jesús stayed, hearing the voices, talking back to them —

(*Note: If one actor is playing* JESÚS *and* NARRATOR TWO, *he is here speaking with a third voice as well.*)

NARRATOR TWO AS VOICE: Jesús —

JESÚS: Padre, de veras estás escuchando a lo que está pasando abajo? (*Are you really listening to what's going on down here?*) Monseñor, el mejor de todos!

NARRATOR/VOICE: Jesús, presente. Estoy aquí.

JESÚS: Sí.

NARRATOR/VOICE: Jesús, I want you to do me a favor.

JESÚS: Mande?

NARRATOR/VOICE: Jesús, tomorrow is Palm Sunday. They are going to hold a funeral for Monseñor in San Salvador. I want you to go up to the mountain, past the wild flowers, and pick the palms there. Those are the ones that Monseñor wants.

JESÚS: No puedo hacerlo. Soy viejo. No puedo aguantarlo. Ask somebody else —

NARRATOR/VOICE: Jesús!

JESÚS: Nobody else, eh? Bueno. Gracias.

NARRATOR TWO: Jesús left the church. Outside, he saw it was the
middle of the night. He went to his house. (JESÚS *does all the next as
described.*) He took off his old work clothes, and put on a poncho he
only wore for weddings, and for funerals: he'd been to a lot of them.
He put on a hat he'd been saving for years, and a bandana against the
chill of the night air in the mountains: he didn't intend to wait for the
sun to rise. Out behind his house, up the twisted trail; he knew the
way in the dark with his feet. Past the plot of ground no longer his, and
through the wild flowers. He went to work by the light of a little moon,
cutting palms for Monseñor. (JESÚS, *with imagined machete, trimming
branches from low palm trees.*)

Something was giving him more strength than he'd had in years; this
made him almost happy —

JESÚS (addressing the VOICE): Okay? Another? Esa?

NARRATOR TWO: And the voice was there —

NARRATOR/VOICE: Jesús.

JESÚS: Sí. Mira lo que estoy haciendo.

NARRATOR TWO: When he'd cut a full load, he lifted the palms on his
back; (JESÚS *shoulders a backload of real palms.*) Still he didn't wait
for sunrise. He started back down the hill. Jesús, walking in the dark,
through the flowers, past the plot of ground with the barbed wire —
he didn't stop at his house now, nor at the church or the plaza. He
started down the road to San Salvador.

(*Instrumental Hispanic/Indian music comes on quietly: evocative of
slow walking, lamentation, night-time.*)

NARRATOR TWO: — and still hearing the voices:

NARRATOR/VOICE: Jesús!

JESÚS: Sí. Mira, allá voy!

(*Short quiet time here: JESÚS walking, the palms on his back rustling,
the music, the feeling of the presence of accompanying spirits.*)

NARRATOR TWO: Jesús didn't know it, but in a great ring all around
San Salvador, nobody could sleep that night. People were getting up,
wrapping their kids in their shawls, and starting out, too: down the

ridge roads, the cliff walks, the old cart tracks — climbing down to San Salvador, for Monseñor. Everyone had lost a father, a mother, children, a teacher, a friend, or a piece of land, a house . . . and now, Monseñor. There were ten thousand, thirty thousand, fifty thousand people that night, making their way to the funeral. Very likely (*to the audience*), had you been living there, you would have been coming down, too. Think of that: you can almost smell the smoldering cooking fires you've left banked behind; you can hear the birds rustling in the trees you pass beneath; you can feel the mists rising from each valley and mixing with your tears.

Jesús was walking alone. Miracles kept happening to him. Every time he almost lost his way in the dark, a hand seemed to push him back on the trail. Every time the load felt heavy on his old back, a hand seemed to reach down and make it light again —

NARRATOR/VOICE: Jesús!

JESÚS: Sí! Voy.

NARRATOR TWO: San Salvador! Daylight. He saw, for the first time, the roads were full of people. Everyone pulled back and made way for the old man with the palms. The marketplace: people waking up. . . . Now he was in the great square with the cathedral; it was packed with people; they all pulled back: make way for the old man with the palms. Make way for Jesús.

The steps of the cathedral. There on the steps, the coffin of the Archbishop, thrown open to the daylight, so the government soldiers would see that this was a funeral, not a demonstration! Jesús felt borne by the press of the people, right up the steps, through the doors, down the aisle, on to the altar — (JESÚS *gently lays down the palms*): — (*Never having stood on an altar before.*)

JESÚS (*looking up*): Okay?

(*The music fades; silent now, the better to punctuate outside noises about to happen —*)

NARRATOR TWO: For the first time, he could straighten up, look around, see where he was — to him the church seemed full of people; it couldn't hold any more, yet more kept crowding in. All the faces seemed turned up toward him: he saw Juancito, Concepción, Marta, Ricardo, Jesuses, too: scores of them, old men from the mountains, crowded into the church — it couldn't hold any more, yet more kept crowding in — for shelter! It was then that Jesús felt what he hadn't before: grief for the Archbishop was no longer the main emotion in that great hall — now it was tension, fright, five thousand bodies trem-

37

bling together. There was a rumor the soldiers had come; nobody knew if they'd get out of there alive.

If you were to reach out now, hold the hand of the person who's next to you — (NARRATOR *waits till the audience does this*) — you might begin to feel what it was like to be in that church, at that time. We in the United States, we live a very comfortable life; we don't know how it might feel to come to a theatre, a church, and know we may never see our homes again.

(*Sounds from outside: bomb explosions, gunfire, crowd noises, soldiers barking orders, theatre doors slamming, locks bolted, spotlight rapidly searching the spectators.*)

NARRATOR TWO: The people in El Salvador live that truth every day. There were soldiers hollering orders, sniper fire, people were dying outside in the plaza, hurling themselves up the steps through the doors; some — old women — were crushed to death inside the church — they couldn't even collapse; there was no room to fall. People were screaming — through the doors came the Archbishop's coffin, held aloft on fingertips, brought in to protect his dead body from the bullets!

(*Noises increase; they quickly fade and are replaced by the sound of a chanting crowd, quiet enough so that the* NARRATOR *and* JESÚS *can be heard clearly.*)

NARRATOR TWO: Jesús, watching those people, he felt their panic, felt their individual power leave them. But it didn't disappear; it seemed to flow through the floor, enter his body, fill him with — he began to speak, to shout, in public for the first time; he had to look down to make sure it was himself speaking!

JESÚS: Hey! This is a funeral! Not a demonstration! Not a battle! Stop the shooting — send the soldiers away! No más! No more! Yo soy Jesús; vengo de la montaña! I just want my land back! Give me back Juancito, Concepción, Marta, Ricardo — ya comprendo! Now I understand! Basta ya! Ya no tengo miedo! Viva Monseñor! No more suffering — revolución o muerte venceremos! The people united —

(SOLDIER *runs in, full dress, sound of gunfire; chant stops*):

SOLDIER: Communeest!

(*He dispatches* JESÚS, *either by gunshot, or wrestling him away. Music up:* JESÚS *vanished, or in death/resurrection tableau.*)

NARRATOR TWO: Archbishop Romero was murdered on March 24, 1980. At the funeral on Palm Sunday, more than fifty people were killed, some by snipers, and some crushed to death in the cathedral. (JESÚS *actor exits.*)

(*Music fades; sound of teletype up. Enter* NARRATOR ONE *as newscaster.*)

NARRATOR/NEWSCASTER:

1980: 100,000 Salvadorans from all walks of life form opposition front to support rebels.
Army murders 600 women and children at Rio Sumpul.
Military sweep: three thousand dead in Morazán.
Four United States women raped and killed by Security Forces.

1981: New U.S. Chief of State, Ronald Reagan, announces Get-Tough-with-Russia policy.
U.S. State Department White Paper calls El Salvador "(*Quote*) . . . A textbook case of indirect armed agression by Communist powers through Cuba."

1982: Salvadoran soldiers come to Fort Bragg to train.
Far right coalition wins election, helped by Madison Avenue advertising firm, McCann Erikson.

Washington Post reveals secret CIA plan for destabilization of the popular revolution in Nicaragua.

1983: Rebels control one fourth of El Salvador, despite bombing raids by U.S. supplied aircraft; total U.S. military aid approaching one billion dollars.

United States arms and trains "Contra" forces for imminent invasion of Nicaragua.

Guatemalan army steps up destruction of traditional Indian village life.

President Reagan re-certifies El Salvador for continued military aid, despite powerful opposition at home, massive human rights violations, and failure to prosecute those in charge of murder of U.S. women.

Ex-Ambassador to El Salvador, Robert White, says: "The foreign policy of the United States today is totally in the hands of the Pentagon and the CIA."

(*Sound of teletype fades*)

Today, (*give date*):

(*The* NARRATOR/BROADCASTER *gives a three-sentence summary of the latest news in the regional war.*)

(*The two actors return to stage center. They pick up and remove the scattered costumes and props:* JESÚS's *hat, dropped at his death, the palms, broom, radio, water jug, his old clothes* — *while* JESÚS's *voice is heard, voice-over*):

JESÚS'S VOICE: Es verdad; el pueblo sigue en lucha. Dijo Monseñor, El gobierno nos puede quitar todo — las casas, la milpa, la vida. Pero siempre hay una cosa que no nos pueden quitar, y eso es: la victoria final! Yo no voy a verla; quizás mis hijos tampoco: pero un día va a cambiar todo — no puede fallar!

The people are still fighting. Archbishop Romero told me: they can take away everything we have, even our life. But there is one thing they can't take away, and that is: our final victory. I am not going to see it; maybe my children won't, either. But one day everything is going to change — it cannot fail!

(*Music up: the song, "El Pueblo Unido Jamás Será Vencido." The actors, who have paused to hear Jesús's final few words in English, stand, bow; they may embrace and dance. Curtain.*)

NOTES BY THE AUTHOR

I wrote the first draft of this play just after directing a production of Euripides' "The Bacchae;" the influence of Greek tragedy is clear. I was — and still am — inspired in every scene by the songs of Victor Jara. I know of no other poet in this century, anywhere on this planet, who has sung such honest and shattering stories in such a sweet voice — the Chilean junta tortured and killed him in 1973 because, I believe, they couldn't deal with his militant sincerity; his gentleness made him too powerful. Victor's songs, and this play, and the works of countless others, are blows struck for clarity amid so much twisting of truth.

By December, 1983, "A Peasant of El Salvador" had been performed about 100 times in 17 states and Great Britain, by the traveling company, Gould & Stearns. The play has changed as it has toured: the text reflects the continuing contributions of Latin American exiles, scholars, and missionaries who have seen it and offered comments. Both Stephen and I have cut some speeches, and written new ones, reflecting what has worked best in performance. The lines spoken by Archbishop Romero are direct quotes from his homilies and press statements; we are grateful to the Unitarian Universalist Service Committee and Maryknoll for rescuing and preserving the tapes of his last memorable Sunday addresses.

Our account of Jesús's final moments in San Salvador is a slight improvisation on history: we borrow from eyewitness reports of Romero's funeral, among them that of Dr. Jorge Lara-Braud, a member of the delegation of U.S. church leaders who attended. We have fictionalized the scene somewhat, to bring a dramatic consummation to Jesús's journey. We have put him *in* the cathedral, whereas he probably would have been on the steps for a longer time. To help the audience feel the fear, we have filled the church with people *before* the panic actually sent them in, but it is conceivable to me

41

that an old man in Jesús's state of suffering, laden with palms and with his sense of divinely-inspired mission, might have walked through the throng and into the church, as we have written it, might have perceived the people coming in as coming to hear him speak. . . . The chant of triumph that the clergy certainly heard becomes, in our play, the single voice of Jesús breaking out and speaking for all.

"A Peasant of El Salvador" is educational drama; hence, every scene is a conscious compromise between dramatic impact and the conveying of information; feedback from our audiences has let us know how well this balance works. The use of narrators is also a deliberate artistic decision: they are familiar, (the rest of the characters are foreigners); they educate the audience quickly in their own language. Narrators increase the sense of conviction and passion in the story, and they report unactable events, as do the messengers in Greek tragedy.

In our production the narrators put on a hat and change a posture, becoming the other characters. In directing the play for two performers, we gain compression: from the small stage area, and from the use of mime techniques such as jump cuts, quick character changes, illusions, and composite gestures. With a larger company, of course the narrators would be separate, though weaving through the action. Women in such a company could play the roles of narrators, television montage, the boy, the TV news broadcaster, and also Concepción, Marta, and María, whose parts, here only suggested, would be enlarged and given speeches.

Finally, you need an actor for Jesús who is comfortable speaking Spanish. In his most relaxed moments, the two languages should mix on stage automatically. Most of the Spanish he speaks is easily understood in the context of the scenes. Where this is not so, it's still all right: hearing the Spanish spoken pleases and empowers the Hispanics in the audience, and it encourages the Anglo population in attendance (who come to love Jesús), to feel comfortable, and not threatened, anywhere they are surrounded peacefully by a language they cannot understand.

Always remember: pronounce the name "Hay-soos!" — one of the most common male names in El Salvador.

The events in this story are real, documented, undeniably true. In our play they become fiction to the extent that we show them all happening to one family. Even so, the tragedy of Jesús, his wife, his children, must pale before the stories of actual tortured families in El Salvador and Guatemala today.

We are grateful to live in the United States. As we travel to our next performance, we delight in the beauty and richness of our land, our farms, our scenic wonders. Arriving in a new town, we are constantly struck by the goodness and gentility of the folk. Everywhere we meet people who are willing and eager to look at Latin America through understanding eyes.

Performing this critical drama is a privilege; we do not take lightly our freedom of speech — our parents fought to protect it, and we yearn to pass it on to our children. Other peoples do not have this privilege — that only makes our responsibility greater.

We firmly believe that the United States is pursuing a course in Latin America dangerous to ourselves, and to the majority of Latin Americans. We cannot police the world, nor should we fight to postpone the empowerment of the poor. Our support for repressive regimes makes us pay an ever more terrible price: we witness the deaths of thousands of potential friends; we kill off the moderate/ progressive forces in those countries who would be our strongest and most attractive allies against any "evil empire;" we push the opposing forces into more extreme and violent camps; we alienate most of the rest of the world; we strain our own resources and tolerance, and we risk a much wider war.

This point of view is not radical, just North-American common sense in the tradition of Tom Paine and Will Rogers. We believe that the people of the United States are ready to support a foreign policy based upon compassion, non-intervention, honesty. We are a powerful country: secure in our wealth, our diversity, our multi-ethnic culture, our sense of humor, we must offer our best to the other countries of this hemisphere (our fair trade, ecological awareness, our running shoes and electric guitars!) — not fear, suspicion, and the threat of force.

The United States is full of men and women who have travelled, lived, and studied in Latin America. They know its cultures, collect the music, love the people and respect their dreams. They are not prisoners of this or that ideology or prejudice. It's time to turn back to them the conduct of our hemispheric affairs.

> —Peter Gould
> Brattleboro, Vermont
> Thanksgiving, 1983

43

SELECTED BIBLIOGRAPHY

(*The Sources marked * directly contributed incidents or narrative analysis to the play.*)

HISTORICAL BACKGROUND (Economics, History, Institutionalized. Terror.)

*Armstrong, Robert, & Shenk, Janet: EL SALVADOR, THE FACE OF REVOLUTION, (Boston, South End Press, 1982.)

*Barnet, Richard, GLOBAL REACH, (Washington, Institute for Policy Studies,   )

Central America Information Office, EL SALVADOR, BACKGROUND TO THE CRISIS, (Cambridge, Mass., 1982.)

Chomsky, Noam, and Herman, Edward, THE WASHINGTON CONNECTION AND THIRD WORLD FASCISM, (Boston, South End Press, 1979.)

Galeano, Eduardo, OPEN VEINS OF LATIN AMERICA, (New York, Monthly Review Press, 1973.)

George, Susan, & Paige, Nigel, FOOD FOR BEGINNERS, (London, Writers and Readers, 1982.)

*Langguth, A.J., HIDDEN TERRORS, (New York, Pantheon Books, 1978.)

Lappé, Frances Moore, & Collins, Joseph, FOOD FIRST: BEYOND THE MYTH OF SCARCITY, (New York, Ballantine Books, 1979.)

ON LIBERATION THEOLOGY & THE CATHOLIC CHURCH IN CENTRAL AMERICA

*Erdozain, Placido, ARCHBISHOP ROMERO, (Maryknoll, N.Y., Orbis Books, 1981.)

*Freire, Paulo, PEDAGOGY OF THE OPPRESSED, (New York, Seabury Press, 1970.)

Gutierrez, Gustavo, A THEOLOGY OF LIBERATION, (Maryknoll, Orbis Books, 1973.)

*Lernoux, Penny, CRY OF THE PEOPLE, (New York, Doubleday, 1980.)

CURRENT REPORTING

American Civil Liberties Union, REPORT ON HUMAN RIGHTS IN EL SALVADOR, (New York, Random House, 1982.)

Collins, Joseph, with Lappé & Allen, WHAT DIFFERENCE COULD A REVOLUTION MAKE? FOOD AND FARMING IN THE NEW NICARAGUA, (San Francisco, Food First, 1982.)

*Oxfam Special Report: Simon, Lawrence, & Stephens, James, LAND REFORM IN EL SALVADOR, (Boston, Oxfam, 1981.)

*Oxfam Special Report: Davis, Shelton, WITNESSES TO POLITICAL VIOLENCE IN GUATEMALA, (Boston, Oxfam, 1982.)

MISCELLANEOUS

Forché, Carolyn, THE COUNTRY BETWEEN US, (New York, Harper & Row, 1981.) (Excellent poetry.)

Rojas Sanford, Robinson, THE MURDER OF ALLENDE, (New York, Harper & Row, 1976.) (The same forces at work in another country.)

CONTINUING EDUCATION

For information updating, please refer to the bi-monthly: NACLA REPORT ON THE AMERICAS, (North American Congress on Latin America, 151 W. 19th St., NY, 10011.)

For intense exposure to some of the economic arguments used in this play: SUMMER INSTITUTE FOR POPULAR ECONOMICS, (apply to: Center for Popular Economics, Box 785, Amherst, Mass.)

TAPE AND DISCOGRAPHY

In the absence of live music, appropriate incidental music for this production is recorded by MONITOR RECORDS, 156 Fifth Avenue, NY NY 10010. Hear especially the music of Victor Jara, Inti-Illimani, Quilapayun, & Grupo Raiz.

Hear also: YOLOCAMBA ITA, Revolutionary Songs of El Salvador, (Flying Fish Records, 1304 Schubert, Chicago, Illinois, 60614.)

For more information about Salvadoran music, and use of the recording of Monseñor Romero, contact Whetstone Books.

Peter Gould and Stephen Stearns have been delighting audiences in New England with their solo and duet shows since 1977. They represented the United States at the 1980 Mexican-International Mime Festival. They have twice won the coveted Vermont Council on the Arts Annual Fellowship Award. The Gould & Stearns repertoire also includes performances of: The Legend of Sleepy Hollow, Jack and the Beanstalk, Pinocchio, a children's mime hour, and the Gould & Stearns Adult Mime and New Vaudeville Show. For information, contact:

Gould&Stearns

RD 2, Box 62   West Brattleboro, VT 05301 802-254-8355